EVERYDAY EPIPHANIES

Everyday Epiphanies

Poems

Mary Lee

Cover design by Shay Culligan

ISBN: 978-1-954353-38-1

Kelsay Books
502 South 1040 East, A-119
American Fork, Utah, 84003

For Anne Dillon
with a heart full of gratitude
for her personal interest throughout
the various stages of *Everyday Epiphanies*

Also by Mary Lee

Bloom

Rejoice Publications, 2016
(an imprint of Matthew James Publications)

Acknowledgments

I am grateful to Roscommon County Council, who selected my work for an Individual Artist Bursary Award in 2017.

My acknowledgments and thanks are due to the editors of the following journals, anthologies, and websites in which some of these poems or versions of them have appeared:

Orbis: "The God of Fire"
Skylight 47 Journal: "Sunny Day"
Presence—A Journal of Spiritual Directors International: "Regard"
The Galway Review 4: "Growth"
Proost Poetry Collection, Reaching for Mercy: "Flame," "Adventus"
Galway Review website: "There is a Kind of Love"
Galway Review website: "Kilclooney Dolmen"
A New Ulster website: "Things I Didn't Know I Loved"
Poems for Patience: "Things I Didn't Know I Loved" (highly commended, 2018)
Face Up to the Sun: "Matins" (Manchester Cathedral Poetry Competition, highly commended, 2019)
A New Ulster website: "Leftovers"
The Anglican Theological Review: "This Poem Takes One Look at You"
Dodging the Rain website: "Breath"
Spirituality: Dominican Publications, Dublin, (various volumes: 2015–2020), "Advent," "Flame," "The Woman at the Well," "Adventus," "Lenten Wish," "Easter People," "Creation," "Send up Flares," "Leftovers," "Reflection on Gib Singleton's Stations of the Cross Sculptures," "Good Friday Pilgrimage," "At the Recovery Centre," "Mary," "Monstrances," "Butterfly"

With warm gratitude, I acknowledge the many people who encouraged me to bring this poetry collection to print: to all the Thursday Skylight 47 poets, past and present, who played a significant part in editing these poems, especially Kevin Higgins, author of several poetry volumes. Kevin's facilitative expertise and insightful editing have greatly impacted the development of my poetry.

I am very grateful to the fine writers who have written endorsements for *Everyday Epiphanies.*

This collection would not be possible without the love and support of my sisters and brothers and their spouses; warm gratitude to my late parents, James and Bridget. To the Mercy Congregation, Western Province, my warm thanks.

Finally, to the many I have worked with and the friends who have inspired me over the years, not least psycho-spiritual writers—especially my late friend, Brendan O'Reilly—your stories and friendships are still in my life.

Contents

Belonging

Seasons of Hope

Seasons

Twigs, stems, branches waltz,
January's biting breeze.
Brittle ones collide
without breaking, subtle
as empathy. Frost-bitten
brambles sparkle; release
tears, moisten earth's crust.

Swaying images contrast
with antennae beneath soil's
cover, safeguarding secrets—
compel contemplation,
the soul's seasons—
under their skin our mysteries
remain.

Shells

Bare, deserted
whelk shell, thumb size,
weathered from the ocean’s

washing; your outer edge
winds like a stair-case.

Each knob, criss-cross vein,
egg-shell texture. Was your abode
a burden or did you hope to find

another home? You take me to yourself
when I lift you from the water’s

edge, Carraroe beach: gaze
into your open door—your hiding place
sends me on a spiral of reflection,

my own thresholds:
shells I’ve shed; selves I inhabit;

my essential self unshed,
more to surrender.

Change

I
Seeds
        fall
into smooth fields,
black layer of earth,
kernels germinate—
    leaves
flowers
    grapes.
Crushing and pressing,
the long, long wait
for whatever enzymes generate—
water always becoming wine.

II
The heart's narrative
inhabits unattended dark,
archive of memory, emotions'
storeroom. Twilight harvests
the psyche's colours—
brings us home to each other.

Easter People

Grief-laden, they find the stone
rolled away; rocks of disbelief
pushed back—

icons fleeing from the sepulchre.
They lift the languished;
urge them to shun entombed life.

When I listen to their witness to a tomb-
turned-womb, I surrender the temptation
to yield—shrivelled hope rises,

buried courage surges—
new grafted to old; startling
surprise hidden in all that is familiar.

Monstrances

Neither canopy nor chants
precede us—no less
his presence whether or not
we file out of church—each of us
our own monstrance, streaming
onto streets, into shops, homes,
hospitals, across playing fields.

He asks a bigger faith: be his face,
welcome strangers to the table;
open the door on prejudice,
make space for the hospitality
of listening, fresh conversations
of promise, despite the wounds
of rupture.

Exodus Echoes

Shrivelled leaves from autumn trees,
energise earth's soil.

You celebrate this falling foliage—
the tree of your life stripped bare
of splendour—insight for others:

you submit to gravity's call, receive vision
from each season's surrender—give thanks

for times of exile, you overcome
oppression's bonds: your efforts endorsed.

Parting of the sea days walking through wistful
waters, you struggle with strange outcomes.

You appreciate those who listen to your life's
wastelands, when turmoil saps
your vigour, resisting chances to warm

indifference. Manna and quail dreams sustain
as November wraps you in abandonment's
wizened leaves. Your fire and cloud shouts

of incredulity once others' assurance places
you on wings for long flights
to unfamiliar destinations.

At the Recovery Centre

for Gina and trafficked women and children
on EU Anti-Trafficking Day
—July 30th, 2018

Gina is guaranteed good earnings
as a bar waitress in Cebu city. Far from
home, she's forced to work in a dark
club with lambent lights. Taken there
under false promises, she's coerced
to join girls with heavy make-up, take
shabu and alcohol.
"Bar fined,"* watchers seize her wages.
Bruises all over her body.

Her life's journey lurches. She suffocates
beneath severe beatings, gestating secrets
while bleak horizons breathe apprehension
and doubts of freedom numb her muscles.

Though broken and bruised she grapples
with divine assurance, clings to the memory
of her grandmother's faith in God
and fighting spirit: she dreams she'll
escape from tyranny's derision
to the Recovery Centre in the city.
She'll find her voice.

*In the Philippines, prostitution is illegal. However, it is legal for a bar customer to pay the bar fine, i.e., a fixed sum paid to the owner of the bar to take a girl away from the bar, usually for sex. The girl is entitled to half the money paid but rarely receives it.

Become body-words of love*

a theologian urges,
although joy and sorrow lurk
beneath your skin's wrinkles.

Temper your attention
to another's changing season;
notice broken loveliness:

confusion's turmoil,
censure's crinkles, cross-
roads of courage; the body's
lines, furrows; elation's sighs.

Love within arm's reach—
observe each other's colour—
ache in eyes, sadness
left behind in smiles.

Shoulders hunched, your heart
groans, knees tremble,
allow tenderness to linger,
listen to your body's wisdom.

Sexuality and the Sacred: Sources for Theological Reflections by James B. Nelson, (Ed.), Westminster John Knox Press, 2nd Edition (2010)

Flame

for Human Rights Campaigners

I wish to celebrate your flame—
the sparkle you contain:
the spontaneous ardour in your breath;

your fingers, ten beacons; your crackle
captivates the sagging spirit
to re-kindle courage; enables

trafficked people face down the spell
of slavery; witnesses their release
from the cavern's trap—you, their

torch to dissipate dark, reach
hearth, respite, freedom. Your allure
attracts others to immerse

in the troubles of the homeless,
facilitates them to perceive the harsh
way power is attained, misery

maintained, saves the displaced.
Your dance delights in destiny's desire.

Lenten Wish

You depart each morning, your boat
on open ocean, mindful that the seas
will bestow what you must handle
and what you won't; you make peace
with knowing very little, amends
with how things are; stunned
when you look at the stars.

Anoint your thoughts with love-breath;
courage your compass; from this perch
cast your hopes as a fisherman's net
—shifting horizons—from this nest
new waters fill your cup; shadows call
for paradise to cover the earth—
the Charter for Compassion
be humanity's greatest attraction.

God of Disguises

The dancing embrace; the comfort
of community; a lover's
return; joy in an overflow

of tears; hunger for oneness
continuous as our heartbeat;
every unmet desire and aches
that yearn for healing.

Last leaves, moonlit sky; stillness
of prayer; scent of roses hanging
in the air; the soft moth's wings;
raindrops, planets; children at play;
the this-ness of each thing.

Tenderness extended hand to hand:
no mistaking the grime on the skin,
fever's flush, the whiff of the unwashed,
the blank eyes of the whacked—
indelibly marked.

In each epiphany you're disguised
and we're surprised, overjoyed.
Distraught at your exhaustion. Your
broken hands and side.

There Is a Kind of Love

after U.A. Fanthorpe

There is a kind of love called nurture
that hugs when tremors threaten;

when turmoil swamps intent, arms
of kindness extend;

when desolation deters vision,
eyes shimmer with wisdom;

when appraisal stifles ordinary effort,
generous offers;

when words are sincere, animating deeds;

when a mother loads up her groceries, holds
her squirmy toddler with an extravagant smile;

when it feels like Winter will never end,
there is a kind of love called nurture
that fills with Spring's beginning.

Growth

Diary

The image on the inside cover
urges: it must be your best
year yet. I need assurance

I'll have the resources
to envisage this urge. No Google
search will pledge how the year
will unfurl, what promises

hope will whisper, which paths
will expand. How to navigate new
rapids; have fortitude for infinity

to evolve beyond boundaries; allow
them be springboards for flight,
or be reconciled to a citizenship
of loss?

My Shadows

You ask how am I—can't complain, I say—
meaning I really want to whinge
about these shadows—how
invisible things prevent me entrusting
others with my soul secrets,
inferiority about failures, weakness.

And still I wonder can shadows
protect me until I can cope:
fear not the strangeness
of the other or hurt that happens
even accidently like volcanos
that bubble up in moments of intensity?

How to forgo the temptation to forget
subversiveness glimpsed; ignore
flaws; put make-up on underworlds
of familiarity? I watch for dark's clarity
to awaken my dawning.

Fire

The way you ignite,
burst into flames,
melts me to the core.

You pour exuberance
over my memories,
embellish my stories,

colour my face,
dance in my eyes,
entice me closer—

tickle my every nerve,
imbibe, enfold me.
I feed you so you

can glow forever.
You replenish me
so that I am more.

Forty Days

Lent seeps into the ground,
colours the crocus—intimates

release. Wild
violets appear in March
grass. Lilac's purple flowering
forecasts Passiontide,

pungent ritual. Lent's long fast
longs to lift a glass
of cabernet, maroon, juicy power.

Out of the tomb
Easter's sacred Bloom.

The Fire I Light Grows into Metaphor

Flames cleanse chimney's gullet;
fluid the air they breathe, breathing
need in me, mysterious as myth.
Orange tongues thrust themselves
into the flue, emerge vapour-blue.

All day the fire sizzles behind
these lines; meanders into my dreams—
the magnifying glass of loneliness
breaks—mingles with the cry of possibility.

Good Friday Pilgrimage

I'm invited to climb Máméan
(The Pass of the Birds) to follow
the way of the Cross. The crowd
trails on rough terrain. April
breeze bites chiller with assent.
Stones roll under foot; the gurgle

of streams accompanies upward
struggle; shadows cause light
to shimmer on neighbouring
summits. An energy flows through
me as if from somewhere else.
Silence surrounds the crowd's
surrender to each Station.

Mary's óchón agus óchón-ó *
resonates through this
wilderness; ears hone to catch
the lyrics' tone. Pilgrims lean into
her lament. Their self-emptying
is not an instant's skill.
His nothingness rustles.

**Alas and alas*-ó from *Caoineadh na dTrí Mhuire*
—Keening/Lament of the Three Marys

Ageing

Bare-branched trees stand
bravely together—yet lonely—
they always made me feel sad
until this morning.

Custodians, holding the fort,
they invite me to see beyond
their still limbs to a benign
horizon; their stark simplicity
motivates me to honour the blemishes
of ageing, self's value without veneer;
each year explore haven't beens
and not yets; chance doing something
outrageous, its fragrance lingering.

Damaged Goods

There's a crack in everything.
That's how the light gets in.
—Leonard Cohen

There's beauty in the broken,
battered, torn. To mend challenges
more than to create. Our brokenness
bids us befriend it, give it time,
mine its depths; wrap it in an embroidery
of storied significance; swim
in its underground rivers, allowing
the ripples to settle themselves.
Bless whole-making with bounty.

Struggle

She glides on tranquil
water, sure of her image.

Fresh surges surprise, unsettle
her poise—strange intrusions

ruffle graceful movement,
immerse her in their turbulence—

she gasps for courage to overcome
        —chokes, reels,

over-turns; unknowingly, finds
her depth, frothing and frazzled.

Now she looks into the sky,
beneath and above.

Growth

The heart's desert,
cave of yearning to be
replete,
blank out
ingratitude;

fill the crevices
with oasis's nourishment:
tears to moisten
parched orifices;

fly with the swallow's
nerve through storms'
scorn to a clement
homecoming, nest

where growth blossoms;
bless and break the clod's
control, mix it with
the soil of understanding
in the garden of enlargement.

Incarnation

Mary

Luke 1: 26-56; 2: 1-20

Something made me say let it be.
Gabriel guaranteed there would
be no end to his kingdom. I didn't
know what he meant.

Don't be afraid, said Gabriel.
It's a blessing, Elizabeth whispered,
held me tight, wiped away my
tears. When I planned to flee,

tantalised by this mystery,
don't be afraid, soothed my mood.
The night before his birth,
resting on a floor, all dense with

animal stench, I remembered the
light I once saw and the words
don't be afraid surrounded me
like a shawl comforting us three

refugees, in strange quarters.
During the night, labour pains
roused me from slumber.
Wonder wrapped around me.

Now he rests on my heart—all
creation pulsing in his temples,
his wrists; he makes me quiver.

I touch his hands, over and over.
Look at his fingers, lift his palms to
my lips, wonder why I was chosen.
He is the image of Joseph.

Messages

in heartbeats
while resting on his
breast, reverberate
through the years,

waken tenderness
like a spray of cherry
blossoms in May,
or a mother bird
protecting her fledglings.

When first told how
his pulse quickened
her core, he traced
his ear until he
received her beat,
pulsing in every vein.

She listens now for the
heartbeat in all things,
the hymn that vibrates
in earth's body.
One Life.

Creation

Suggested by Sieger Koder

Womb—dark blue orb,
billions of light years,
splendid sphere birthed
into space.

Open hands reveal earth's
profusion—humans centre
stage; brooding wings hover,
receptive hand mothers
in the shelter of dove's wings.

Fruits, grain, flowers; mother, father,
child. Ephemeral and durable
side by side; butterfly's elusive
beauty, layers of Jurassic rock.

Do the dark, flecked edges suggest
that all is not well?
Is the greening of forests at risk?
the family of the future defenseless?
Red roses and poppies, passion

and suffering: war, want,
abundance, sensual thirst; wheat,
grapes, water, baby at the breast,
the beloved, One of us.

Incarnation

A dying woman fills my eyes.
A homeless man holds out his hand
for a meal. A jobless lone mother
frets about her health and her
children's hunger.

I perceive myself in these encounters
from a variant, expanded angle,
grateful to them for their reminder
I often overlook through haste
clouding my lenses.

I make my way to church, receive
an infusion of enthusiasm—Advent
songs, long for Christmas—
celebration of our divinity; turn
to Christ, whose love messages I'm
still learning to read—how each
divine arrival needs work, balm, asylum.

Echo of Dust

I
All beings have their origin
in the ocean. Tears regenerate
allow us taste the saltwater
of life; are a means

to encounter the desert within:
feel fears, smallness, the dark
chaos; give the angels a chance
to feed us.

II
Cinderella girl spends lonely times
in ashes, subdued, dutiful, smudged,
waiting, before she knows her beauty,
marries, goes to the great feast.

III
Remember you are dust
and into dust you shall return.
Remember, remember, remember.

Someday blown in the wind,
the actions of your soul abide.
Blackened thumbs press the sign
of the cross on foreheads.

Butterfly

Psyche, the Greek name for soul,
the same for butterfly.
Life begins when it bursts from the tomb
of an egg laid on a leaf.

The caterpillar eats its birth leaf;
dull, grovelling life, expands though
moulting, sheds its outgrown skin again
and again; chubby, no wings, seems
asleep—busy within, rapidly changing
into chrysalis.

Organs, tissue, limbs metamorphosed,
a red admiral is born.
After rest, pumps blood into its wings
gets them to flap in four hours;

Fluttering beauty in the blaze of day.
Souls familiar with growth's travail,
refined by imaginings rise from the night,
tender throbbing.

Send up Flares

I
You reach back
to that primal burst:

fire of sun,
fire of earth,
fire of birth.

Be spark
thrower, be immensely
brave, send up flares,

fierce with flame
of fortitude.

II
Close your eyes, let your
every cell pulse;
surrender to sensitivity's
promptings.

Each of you
touches another; together you
colour each morning,
beacon all over the cosmos.

Reflection on Gib Singleton's Stations of the Cross Sculptures

(Prayer Garden, St. Francis Cathedral, Santa Fe, New Mexico)

I
Condemned to death.
Moment of decision,
moment of grace.

II
The cross is laid on His shoulders—
He holds the strain of our tomorrows.

III
He falls the first time: His shadow
comforts.

IV
His mother in the crowd—
their souls meet—here all borders
end and begin.

V
Simon relieves His shoulder's weight.

VI
Though He falls again—falling's
as necessary as the hands
that raise up the fallen.

VII
Veronica gentles His face into a towel.
She sees without being seen—can't
touch without being touched.

VIII
He speaks to the invisible women—
one arm open to affirm them, seamless
garment in the other—the one His
mother gave him.

IX
He falls the third time; dissolves delusions
and fears born of our estrangement;
touches the jagged edges of our fissured hearts.

X
In the sludge; stripped of His garments
and more: His second skin.
Though the soldier looks as if to console
he withholds, altering history.

XII
The soldier's body-gesture mirrors
what could be a gentle scene: does
violence border intimacy?

XII
Their bodies arc as if the soldier
is about to take Him into his arms—
alas, his hammer's thrust crushes
Love's limbs.

XIII
His mother, listens to his last breath.
Clasps his dead weight in her lap.

XIV
His descent beneath earth's crust:
the way upwards—spanning horizons.
He falls into the Other's embrace.

Unreachable

On the *Arts* corridor, patients
pass to appointments: aching
joints etch expressions; indelible
wrinkles expose imperceptible
wounds. Who among this retinue
of passers-by is threatened
by a daunting diagnosis; who longs
for a dawn of promise, wholeness,
healing; for whom is loneliness
so intense that it eclipses all other
sentiment?

Their profiles haunt—I hold each of them
in hidden arms; I want to be their breath,
breathe out anything that averts fear,
pray they be buoyed by some breath
from beyond.

The things we'd love to do
for others, often unreachable,
become memories.

Written after *Poems for Patience* Launch
University Hospital, Galway, 2019

The God of Fire

spells crucifixion, extends to the heart where no eye or hand reaches.

Flaming torch of love, suffering, destruction renews trees that require fire to survive. Intense heat melts the cones of the ponderosa pine, sealed with resin, disperses their seeds that germinate in the ash beds.

Like a lion that never expires, the god of fire roars, arrives into your life in ways you wish you could avoid; flames, leaps, dances; the god of the *burning bush not consumed* wants to hold your gaze; his warmth and yours the same brightness.

He sifts and sorts the things you hide even from yourself; brings out the monsters with springs in their steps, taunting your colours, talents and limitations as when a chemist tells the essentials by the flame's shade: yellow, ochre, lilac, crimson, apple-green...

the core of your body opens through the heat of love's fire.

Breath

Inhabitor of the invisible.
Each in-take from
the reservoir
of who knows where;

essential
from birth-cry
to bye-bye;

verve of spirit, vibes,
voices that sway
and those un-heard.

Breath goes where it wills,
releases doubt,
energises desire.

Breath,
ex-haler of failures,
inhaler of freshness,
buyer of time.

Regard

So then assemble me—tell me your favourite
memories of our sojourn. Build from fragments
maps that guide us forward to each other.
What new outlooks will we summon?
What collages will we create of the way it could
have been, had our love known its depth; had we
had courage to push the frontiers of honesty?

Let us assemble each other; hear compassion's
call with tenderness, savour tastes of tolerance,
welcome discord with regard. Convert crises to
contriteness; strike our own note; release
even respectable self-agendas; tether escapist
tendencies; be buoyed by each other's abundance;
thrive in the garden of kindness.

Creator

Silent the dark where all life
begins. Time creates
you and all generations.

Born of original energy:
seed, hydrogen,
helium, iron.

You ascend to the light—
its fingerprints on moss,
grass, flower. You wake

to the hunger for nourishment;
consume its ancient story,
flesh, blood, bone, thirteen
billion years growing.

You mirror Trinitarian self-giving;
refilling. Universe's vigour
exchanged in each cell's relationship.

Like a musician's improvisation,
you resemble imagination
shaping the world.

A Room with a Table and Fire

our worlds begin and end here,
ambiance
softening squabbles.

Food carrying us on roads
within and without. Our imaginings
drink tea with us, recall gifts,
enemies, the ghosts of our
forebears: famine

in our bones for the way she died
on the boreen
between us and our neighbour's holding,
carrying an egg
for her starving family.

We hide in her heart's spaciousness;
weep for the terror of her death.

Comes a Time

Tiny circular blankets rest on the tops
and edges of bushes, cover grass.
Autumn moisture displays
images, concealed resilience:

each morning fresh engineering
feats—exquisite artistry. Alas my
exodus by the gate undoes in seconds
what took the spiders hours to create.

Comes a time when life can't retrieve
its original relief, old road-maps obsolete;
when the web can't be restored,
when the flood carries away every
cherished reminiscence,
the fire leaves nothing save ashes.

What permits us be resilient
in a cramped cranium, life straining
to originate a hub network where
the new ordinary thrives?

Ordinary Time

Chores

I dream of flying free above
the trap of gravity. Each day
in the ocean of the ordinary, undramatic,
existence on autopilot; chores
and tired attitudes accumulate.

Does dullness prune the ego?
Do I measure myself by small choices,
burdened tracks, tried and reliable,
or by the miracle of special moments,
or some intermingling of the two?

Trauma meets transfiguration
in the lacework of my life. The strangeness
of silence seeded with recognitions:
loss of security jolted; a friend's looming
demise; kindness in another's eyes;
my narratives of desire.

Silence

So much of what we live is left unsaid—
the records of loss, unseen tears—
the silent aches of love; fertile
Summers faded, shrinkage

of years in the skin's wrinkles.
What we hide is always more than what
we confide—everyday epiphanies,
our uncharted cathedrals—
unrecognised.

After Psalm 23

You replenish my spirit
with the sun's exuberance—
colour and smell of heaven,
more than my soul can
behold on its own.

Your immensity once walled
in a womb seals space and spell.
You animate prairies; paint
daisies; honeysuckle all
Summer, even their drooping
beauty, a wonder.

Stillness or storm's display,
your breath in my hair.
I hear your name in the rain,
dive into your tide, relax by your
side; pride in our intertwining;

flourish in your focus, ache
when your pain echoes in my
bones; you cleanse cells
and muscles; secretly your
breath floats under my skin.
You glisten when the wick
of my conviction thins.

The Presence Who Tames

> *You become responsible forever for what you have tamed.* Antoine de Saint Exupéry

Your taming bids me into being
with every spoken and written word.
Let me call you in with these:
each breath peppering the air; each
heartbeat and the vital heat of laughter.

Tame me when Spring's vigour summons me
to touch roots; in Summer, to feast
on your miracles: stunning Calla Garnet Glow;
Stella Maris rose;
Sweet Pea's generous show.

In Autumn tame me to trust ripening;
instil moments of assurance
when loneliness in lengthening shadows
lurks and dark's embrace
cautions the nourishment of dreams.

Winter, as my friend—so like me
now—his age when he collapsed; hold
me as I did him, then. Tame me like his
voice—music quickening my joy, glistening
my wonder—knowing I held his life.

Plenitude

Communion bread is placed into
my hand. Outside church blackberries burst
into their tender selves on the walkway's
thrusting brambles.
          The water I rinse them in
blushes—I imbibe symbol and substance.
Incarnation imbues my flesh.

In the dark of night I see rivers running red;
drink colour from the day: water, wine,
wafer; smell the sum of Fall's profusion.
I strike a match to a candle—words
endorse the whole season in my mouth.

Dandelions

Yellow pests on Spring's green
blanket greet mornings
with confidence; evenings
the blooms rest
on leaf pillows.

I try to uproot them,
eradicate their impertinence.
Change my mind for the bees'
sake and the plants' esculence:
roots, leaves, flowers:
medicine, wine, nectar, dye.

Three celestial bodies
in their lifecycle: yellow
blaze for sun, puff-ball,
the moon, dispersing
seeds, the stars. The lawn
ablaze with buoyancy.

Thirst

An energy called thirst
makes us cry at birth; never
stops surging—body for
restoration—soul for succour.
Our eyes are colour-thirsty,
our ears are news-thirsty; our
tongues tied for speech.

When we pause,
grow older our thirst
intensifies for the liquid of love
because of loneliness—
the liquid our thirst needs.

Kilclooney Dolmen

Stone aperture,
it holds

a door's step to the mountains,
a red-dark sky

and my long, long look
into silence.

Matins

This too is prayer:
bare branches allowing the sun to stream lighthouse beams;
the woodpecker on her oak tree;
swans and four cygnets;
stillness;
first stirrings: a snail, house on back reaches the grass verge;
robins from branch to branch;
fog over rolling hills;
lanes shimmer;
fragrance of rain;
beads on wire fencing;
the embrace of air;
blue meadows of morning sky;
waves warmed in ochre orange.

Buttery blooms on agile stems gush
exuberance. I imbibe nature's matins,
daily in my paradise.

Leftovers

On my table steaming soup:
a bowl of truth from minced
meat, vegetables, purées.

The world of commerce requires
me to believe this is just soup,
commodity to be consumed.

I know farmers
who grow and harvest produce—
the sacrifice my nourishment
signifies. I am indebted to them.

Unjustly treated garners of kidney
beans and corn visit my conscience
when I look into a saucer of this salad.

My hunch is my lunch shares
in the structures that keep others
hungry—workers whose children
can't afford a meal today, keep

their pangs to themselves. In this
moment of full and plenty, nourished
by leftovers, I savour all life, from
soup to succour with gratitude.

Conspiracy

On my walk I'm arrested
by a mound of seaweed. Striving
to define its precise shade, I fall
into sky and deep blue sea.

A seagull still in the wind rests
in its silhouette, then soars higher:
I'm lifted aloft, span bushes bejewelled
with berries, apple trees' green and red

baubles. I swallow blackberries till their dye
leaks through my skin; make a fascinator
from heather and pigeon's feathers.
This conspiracy of images envelops me.

Driftwood

River sculpts the landscape,
winks at me from its bed; mountains
and valleys backdrop—purple
and sage shadings—land speaking

beauty to eye and hand. I gather
driftwood scattered on Corrib's shore,
propelled and shaped by waves'
Summer glory. It hangs on a nail

in my kitchen high above the stove,
in its graceful simplicity—
the whole universe imprinted
with patterned intricacy—indelible fingerprints.

November Memos

Wrapped in the newspaper
of the ordinary, muted epiphanies
displayed in every bush, pond, bud.

Though a coma of cold envelops
earth, nature's travail burgeons
beneath—snowdrops' milk-white
mantles must appear.

Twigs intertwine, trees bereft
of leaves reveal tiny buds—
silhouettes in a baby-blue horizon.

Sun slants through windows, sends
gilded dimples into pools of rainwater—
turquoise, orange, crimson

crawl across the skyline, glint
on shrivelled leaves, lift their expiry
in the mud to kaleidoscope—November
memos entrusted to nature's mulch.

Things I Didn't Know I Loved

after Nazim Hikmet

I always knew I loved silent moments when
wonder creeps up beside me with a nudge—
a cup of coffee—
the steam warming my face
like the scent of a lavender candle.

I always knew I hated
qualms clanging in the background
that rob me of the luxury to exhale;
flimsy deceptions of resistance, habits
of distraction when I care too much
what others countenance me to be.

I always knew I loved tiny theophanies:
hues in eyes, transformative smiles;
the sound of rain on window panes;
bare trees; a warm bedspread;
the wonder of hot water on leaves
and ground beans; the smell of baking bread.

I always thought I wouldn't like wine
until my initiation. I always knew
I didn't like jostling crowds, embodied
smells and loud bells during gathered worship
until I realised these are harbingers
of transcendence to alert attention's dimness.

Belonging

Hope

A sea-crossing—where
you arrive depends on the winds
and the ocean; on disclosures
that waken. Your navigation

hinges on how you inhabit
the mystery you are, your
alertness to the elements'
imminence, your freedom

to be hurt:
step out of the boat
onto the turbulence, knowing
if anything can hold your weight,

your attention can—
eyes fixed on that original quest.
You don't know where your
conversations will take you:

what will be evoked in you—
perhaps your loneliness
will lead you to be more
courageous—risk yourself

to experiences' hazards, find
the home of your belonging,
make promises you can keep, take
the hand you know belongs in yours.

The Woman at the Well

suggested by Siegar Koder

Outcast.
She stands at the well gazing.

Dark.
Deep water.
Meets a man;
they sit together
at the well's cap-head.

The sun's noon-day heat
frames her countenance.
The water mirrors their encounter.

What wells of her meanderings
does she draw from
while she stares into these depths?

She cringes, changes the subject;
looks away ashamed.

Is she a victim of levirate marriage
with no choice of partners,
or a woman of shady ways?

Sunny Day

You saunter aimlessly
at the sea's rimmed mystery:
flow, ebb, alteration,
tranquility.

Fear with freedom treads
on the strand of
thresholds; silver shells,
white webs on the shingle

mingle with the sky's
image on ocean's edge—
each new cloud says
you have seen, been

seen, and nothing is ever
as it seems—your reflection
a wordless moment, mirror
of light—the dance of light-beams.

June 2016

Mountains, solemn, solid, unchanging
except for hue ranges, lavender, blue.

Mint-green pastel shades
configure on calm waters.

Sunny spells on lazy waves
shimmer like lapis lazuli.

Shafts of sporadic sunshine on fields
with amber spangles.

Hypnotic aromas, honeysuckle,
hay, meadowsweet.

Oak trees, sycamore, maple,
heavy with leaves.

Some mornings grey mist drapes
the mountains, fills the hollows.

You recognise there is a world you
can't sense, hear, know.

The eye knows more than the beholder
can hold.

This Poem Takes One Look at You

And all it wants is to call you Pristine.
Pristine hands, their touch and pulse.
Pristine face, unfolding towards the sun.
Pristine feet and everything in between.

Pristine even in pain and disarray.
In shame, pristine still.
Pristine in delight, morning light
emanating from your core.
Pristine being born.
Pristine when laid down at death's hour.

Two Movements

The waves roll over into one another,
indistinguishable,
    inimitable.
Rise
      Fall
            Die
Rise again;
unrepeatable surge—
invisible urge.

Tide crawls between pebbles,
chucks, among rocks—
spreads white webs
hissing on damp, dark sand.

Meanwhile
the waves gather themselves.
Tidal energy cleanses
away hindrance; buoyant
white heads bow to blueness.

Love's ever-restless wave rides
relationship's squalls, rocks
in the heart thaw.

This Is My Body

I apply moisturiser
to my sunburned arms and legs.
The words this is my body
flood my being—a light gleams
and I see my flesh as if for the first
time. Sometimes words
and the moment merge, beget
fresh meaning.

My body—receptacle
of memory, registrar of pain
delight, slights and dreams.
No ordinary thing—my most
hidden being—frontier
with the unknown.
Maimed, forlorn or healthy,
I awaken daily, beloved.

This is my body, perspiring
in midday heat, parched
with thirst, breathless
at the sight of a sunset, soft
and searching until flesh
breathes into this poem.

There's a Word

and I don't yet know it:
when you rest

your eyes in mine and I
can only guess your desire

your whisper
I can't define—its longing
called me long ago

your touch tingling
my skin, makes me tremble
in this room of stillness

your silent sadness I
want to heal, soothe
each wound.

There's a word for these moments
when my listening body hears.

Gift

in memoriam Kindred Spirit, Friend

The river of your voice silenced.
Still your presence leaves a familiar
scent. You seem to breathe and live
everywhere. New messages emerge
from your absence:

where old tracks are lacking
a new terrain unfolds its wonder;
my outer shell melts under memory's spell.

Shrubs cast aside their colourful shawls,
tree twigs shrug away their issues.

Strange how death turns to gift and yet
I know it so. Some transformations
are slow, not easily earned but worked
from grim stone.

About the Author

Mary Lee's poetry has been widely published, including in the following books, journals, and websites: *Skylight 47; Crannóg; Orbis; The Poet's Quest for God* (Anthology, Eyewear Publishing, UK); *The Anglican Theological Review; The 2018 Poiema Series* (Anthology); *Poems for Patience Competition; The Linnet's Wings; Time of Singing; The Galway Review* 4; *The Furrow; Dodging the Rain* website; *Presence: A Journal of Spiritual Directors International; Proost* (Collection 2); *Spirituality:* Dominican Publications; *Adam, Eve & the Riders of the Apocalypse* (Wipf & Stock); *Face Up to the Sun,* (Manchester Cathedral Publications); *A New Ulster* website; *The Wild Word* website; *The Galway Review* website. Her work has been broadcast on RTE Radio 1, *A Living Word,* and her poems have been cited at liturgies and retreats.

Originally from a farm on the shores of Lough Corrib, Mary lives in Galway. She writes poetry as an expression of gratitude for the myriad experiences and revelatory moments in nature and in social, church, and community circles.

Praise for *Everyday Epiphanies*

You cannot isolate *eros* from *agape*, the sensual Creation from the embodied human spirit. But it takes a life of scars and starlight to learn this by heart.

This is perhaps why *Everyday Epiphanies* favours in-between times, cusps and sea-changes, the shape-shifts of the seasons, and the shoreline itself.

Loss and discovery, the lively and the lethal, shadow and suntrap, are always intermingled in these verses. Seepage is everything. Our first of Spring is still the English winter, and the Fall is still a harvest festival.

Here, then, are hymns to a hyphenated world, as in Lee's lovely Nativity poem, "Mary"

I touch his hands, over and over.
Look at his fingers, lift his palms to
my lips, wonder why I was chosen.
He is the image of Joseph.

—Aidan Mathews, award-winning poet, playwright and novelist, and producer, RTÉ

~

In her new poems, Mary Lee presses ever deeper into the mysteries of existence through the portal of the quotidian. The collection invites the reader toward a contemplative acceptance of what *is*—a giving up of control and a seeking to love better: to love God, neighbour, Other, self, the body, the earth and its wild abundance, the changing seasons, change itself, including the inevitably painful losses. "…I'm/still learning to read – how each/divine arrival needs work, balm, asylum," she writes in "Incarnation," as indeed the divine arrival of this book instructs the soul in the unique contours of all three.

—Daniel Bowman, Jr, Associate Professor, Department of English, Taylor University. Editor-in-Chief, *Relief: A Journal of Art & Faith*

~

In *Everyday Epiphanies,* Mary Lee writes with passion and joy, making room in this packed collection for the loves and losses, the people and places, the joys, and griefs that mark life's journey. Grounded in a sensitivity to sound and rhythm, the poems move from an awareness of the senses to an attention to the "broken loveliness" of the sick, the indigent, the trafficked, the oppressed; and from a keenly felt joy in nature to a sense of our interdependence with the whole community of life. Readers can relish such memorable lines as "Brittle ones collide/without breaking, subtle/as empathy" and "the blemishes/of aging, self's value without veneer." They can enjoy the surprising realization that a water bird looks "into the sky/beneath and above." They can walk with fresh eyes into scriptural landscapes, see Mary examine her baby's "fingers, lift his palms to/my lips," consider the "love messages I'm still learning to read" from Christ or follow the Stations of the Cross anew. Throughout this assortment of poems, readers will find much to inspire them. They may share the poet's hope that such fragments may be 'maps that guide us forward to each other.'

—Mary O'Connor RSM, author of *Windows and Doors* (poetry, 2012) and *Their Circle of Mercy* (cultural history, 2019)

~

This book of poems expresses Christian spirituality in a far more intimate and revealing way than is possible from a pulpit or a rostrum. The messages are at once simple, liberating, and forthright. Each poem calls us to stop, to consider, and to see the beauty and sacredness of everyone and everything around us. The poet finds God in all of life and all of life in God. In her poetry there is no duality, no separation; everything is holy, everything is one. If you choose to read a poem every day, I suggest it be from this collection where you will find each of them will speak to what you want to see in yourself. This book deserves to be read by everyone.

—Sr. Stanislaus Kennedy, RSC, well-known social justice campaigner and social innovator. She is also a meditation teacher and an author of several bestselling books on social and spiritual themes.

~

I particularly liked the Stations Sequence: "He holds the strain of our tomorrows," "His shadow comforts," "falling's / as necessary as the hands / that raise the fallen," etc.

"Unreachable" really reverberated with me. Lines like "I hold each of them / in hidden arms" are wonderful. "This is My Body" sees things from a marvellous angle, and "There's a Word" repays much re-reading.

—Padraig Daly, OSA, author of several poetry collections and translations from poets writing in Irish and the Italian poet Edoardo Sanguineti.